I0201059

I Want Ice Cream, Please

I Want Ice Cream, Please
Lessons Learned from Our Autistic Son

by Dana Pride

Everlasting Publishing
Yakima, Washington
USA

I Want Ice Cream, Please
Lessons Learned from Our Autistic Son
by Dana Pride

Drawings by Nathan Pride
Cover Art by Jahla Brown

ISBN: 978-1-7348047-2-0

First Edition
Everlasting Publishing
PO Box 1061
Yakima, Washington 98907
USA

©2021 by Dana Pride
All rights reserved

For Nathan, Jahla, Mom and Dad, and my husband, Rev. Willlie F. Pride, Jr.

I Want Ice Cream, Please
Lessons Learned from Our Autistic Son

Introduction

I started writing this book when our son, Nathan, was 13. I had planned a very short book with some of his drawings to accompany ten life lessons I've learned from Nathan. I soon discovered two more lessons, and I couldn't leave any of them out of the book. As I finished typing up the lessons, I knew I had to tell Nathan's story. These weren't merely lessons that popped out of an unknown or generic boy. These lessons came from our boy, our son, and to understand the meaning behind the lessons, the reader should get to know the boy. Life happened, Nathan grew, and I learned more from him as years passed.

The book is now in three parts, with drawings by Nathan throughout the book. Part 1 introduces you to Nathan, starting at his birth and going through his teens. Part 2 is a poem I wrote as I imagined what was going on inside his mind. Part 3 contains lessons I have learned from him. If you want to skip right to the lessons, go straight to Part 3. But I hope you'll get to know Nathan first.

Part 1

Our Nathan

It's a boy! I am holding our new baby, looking into his dark eyes, admiring his fat cheeks and all that brown hair plastered to his head, thankful that he is okay. Labor had been long, and the doctor had called for an emergency C-section when he ascertained that the umbilical cord was wrapped around our baby's neck. Although I did have my heart set on a natural birth, after going through 14 hours of painful contractions in the birthing room, I am relieved to be offered an end to my pain. Now the pain is over, and we are alone in the hospital room with Nathan, the newest and most beautiful baby in the world. My husband, our daughter and I are so excited about this black-eyed little member of our family. All his vital signs and infant tests are fine on this perfect tiny boy.

When he is two days old, before we come home from the hospital, I notice his eyes have turned blue! They were almost black when he was born, now they are blue.

3

Nathan is now two months old, ready for his first checkup. He has never smiled. As a matter of fact, all he has wants to do is to nurse for hours on end, and I don't have enough milk to satisfy him. He frowns and looks grumpy all the time. A month ago, we began adding bottles of formula between nursing times, which he drains in about a minute. He has been fussy, crying, frowning, never sleeping more than an hour at a time. The sound of the footsteps of our cat, Punkin, walking on the carpet into his room is enough to awaken the light-sleeping Nathan. I spend nights holding him, rocking him, taking him out on the deck to get fresh air, but he will only sleep for a short time before waking, crying.

At Nathan's 3-month checkup, his doctor gives us what turns out to be the most wonderful advice when he tells us, "Nathan is hungry. Give him baby formula with cereal in it." After his first bottle of formula fortified with cereal when we get home from the doctor appointment (and grocery store), Nathan finally sleeps through the night! He begins to smile, and he becomes the happiest baby I have ever seen. All this time, he has been hungry! Now he is finally getting full, and he is so smiley and happy all the time.

At 8 months, Nathan is very aware of where I have my attention. When he is near enough to touch me and I am not looking at him, he turns my face toward him. He wants constant eye contact with me, or to know I am watching him. His little arm is so strong as he turns my head in his direction!

Now his eyes have changed to green. The rest of us have brown eyes. Perhaps he got his green eyes from my mother.

One

At one year, Nathan can do a sit-up when lying on his back, without using his hands! He does a sit-up in his crib, sits there, satisfied, and looks around the room, watching us. He is not yet walking or talking. He doesn't cry any more. I wonder how his voice will sound when he begins to talk? I try to not compare him with his sister, who began talking at eight months, and took her first step at eleven months (on my mother's birthday). In general, girls start talking and walking earlier than boys do. At his one-year checkup, his doctor tells us Nathan is developing perfectly physically. He is very happy and healthy, and we have nothing to be concerned about. He is smiling and chubby, content to sit and watch his family members who are in the room with him.

His hearing is excellent. We nickname him 'Fox Ears.' He is aware of every sound, even many sounds that I can't hear or automatically dismiss. He hears when the downstairs door closes (the rest of us can't hear it) and he looks in the direction of the stairs, getting excited when Daddy arrives home. When he hears loud sounds, his hands fly to his ears, and he cringes and gives me a pained look, as if he is physically being injured.

Up until his first birthday, we have not given Nathan any food with sugar in it. On his birthday, we introduce him to ice cream and cake. He loves ice cream! He doesn't really care for cake, but he does like the frosting.

Since he hasn't started talking and I know Sign Language (I have worked at a school for the Deaf for 16 years), I teach him some signs. He is very interested when the signs have to do with food. He quickly learns and uses signs for 'milk,' 'ice cream,' 'juice,' 'Mama,' and 'Daddy,' but he mostly ignores all other signs.

Shortly after Nathan's first birthday, on a Sunday morning, he seems to be having a hard time breathing. I think he might have a cold. He is cooperative as we get him ready for church. We go to church, and he keeps breathing loudly all day. He is not crying or fussing, his breathing is just labored. The next day his breathing has not improved, and he is wheezing. I go to work, and my husband takes him to the doctor. Around nine o'clock, I am in a meeting when I get a call from my husband. The doctor tells him to take Nathan straight to the hospital!

My heart is pounding as I rush to meet them at the hospital, where Nathan has already been admitted and is in a room. He's in a crib and he has a breathing contraption attached to him – and he is not struggling to breathe now. The doctor tells us he thinks Nathan has RSV, respiratory syncytial virus, which is common in babies and young children. I have never heard of it. The treatment for Nathan is to be hooked up to a breathing machine every hour so he can inhale some medicine. I stay at the hospital with him all week, and he is awake most of the time, happy to have me in his room with him.

On Friday, his breathing is completely normal again, and he is discharged from the hospital. We get a prescription for a nebulizer (a pump-thing that attaches to a nose-and-mouth cover) and albuterol (a tiny bottle of liquid that we pour into the nebulizer for him to inhale). By now, after watching the nurses do this all week, we are familiar with how to attach and use this device. We are to use it any time he begins to struggle to breathe. We end up using it a few times during the next couple of years.

Nathan has a great sense of direction. When we are driving home from church, he leans over and watches through the front window from his car seat, to see if we are turning to the right, towards McDonald's (he LOVES ice cream!) or to the left, towards home. When we turn to the right, he gets excited, clapping his hands. When we turn to the left, he gives a little whine of complaint. He rarely falls asleep in the car, even on long drives: he is constantly watching to see where we are going.

Two

At the age of two, Nathan is starting to walk, but he still is not talking. When he walks, he is careful and deliberate with each step. Where the carpet ends or changes to a different pattern, he slows to a stop and is very cautious stepping from one surface to the other. He seems to have trouble with depth perception when the floor or ground changes from one visual pattern to another. He uses his foot to test the new area, where it is, if it is higher or lower than the current level. We know – from experience? – that the level is not changing, but he is just learning this.

At his two-year checkup, we ask Nathan's doctor about his development. He tells us not to worry since Nathan is so happy and progressing well. Physically, he is developing the same as other 2-year-old boys, a bit taller and a bit thinner than most, but his mental development is more like a one-year-old. The doctor tells us he will most likely catch up soon. I can't help but wonder if his development is behind by one year or behind by one half? - but it doesn't matter. I am thankful that he is such a cheerful and joyful boy.

Nathan has not babbled like most babies do, but I sing to him every day. I sing all the nursery rhymes, and I make up songs about what we are going to do, such as, "We are going bye-bye in the car, going bye-bye, yes, we are! We are going bye-bye in the car, yes, we are!" He loves when I sing to him. He loves music, at home, in the car, and at church.

All the time, he is quiet, smiling, watching and listening what everyone else is doing and saying. He also is fascinated by watching his reflection in the mirror and the sliding glass door. He often goes to the mirror and he is doing something, as he is standing, watching himself, in a world of his own. He moves his hands, watches his expression and occasionally stomps his foot. He seems to be playing a game, he is so captivated by his reflection.

Nathan had his second birthday three months ago. His grandmother, my mother-in-law, is visiting us from Detroit and he really loves her. He is always happy, but when he is with his grandmother, he is simply delighted. When she and I go into the kitchen to fix dinner, Nathan comes with us and goes straight to the sliding glass door to start playing his game, watching his reflection. I tell Grandma Jackson that he is doing something. She watches him for a minute, and she knows exactly what he is doing. "He's preaching," she says. She is correct! He is imitating his daddy, who is a pastor. I am so glad to finally know what Nathan has been doing! He watches himself, stomps his foot at the appropriate times, like a good Baptist preacher, while holding a toy flashlight to his mouth that I now recognize as his microphone – yet he still is not speaking a word or making a sound.

During the summer, I go out of town for a few days on a work trip. When I return, Nathan shows his appreciation for me by immediately following every direction I give him. He needs his diaper changed, so he quickly lies on the floor and puts his feet up. When I tell him it is time for dinner, he goes straight to his high chair so I can put him in it. For one week after I return, he is very responsive and obedient. He seems to be connecting his obedience with my being at home with him; but I have no idea if he has a concept such as good boy = mommy home.

In August, we drive across the state to visit my mom, Nathan's other grandmother, for the weekend. Nathan has been healthy and hasn't needed to use the nebulizer for about ten months; but when we wake up on Sunday morning, Nathan is wheezing loudly. I didn't bring the nebulizer with us – it didn't occur to me that he might need it this weekend. I take him to the emergency room, which is pretty busy for a Sunday morning. I am holding Nathan and he is getting heavy, but I can't put him down; he is struggling breathe! When I get to the front of the line and explain that my baby can't breathe, the receptionist tells me in a bored manner to take a seat and she'll get to us soon, we have to wait our turn.

I tell her frantically, "He can't breathe!"

She asks, "Is he throwing up?"

"No."

"Then he has to wait his turn."

As I step away from the reception desk, Nathan makes the loudest retching sound, as he turns his head away from me and vomits all over the floor. The receptionist calls for a special code over the loud speaker, and suddenly eight nurses and assistants are surrounding us and rushing us into a room, attending to Nathan, placing him on a bed, hooking him up to oxygen and calling for a doctor to come right away.

I explain that he has RSV but he hasn't had an episode in nearly a year. Nathan is fine after his nebulizer treatment, and they release him. We go back to my mom's house to gather our things, then we drive back across the state to our home. I make a mental note to always carry the nebulizer with us when we travel. Nathan only needs to use it a couple more times during the year, then he never needs it again after he turns 3.

Three

Nathan is three now. I have begun to document his progress in a notebook. He has a speech/language delay, and his hearing has tested as normal. He is finally experimenting with his voice, attempting a couple of words, and to sing the alphabet song, but with many gaps in his formation of sounds. He says "ca" for cake or ice cream; "gaga" for Daddy; "hu-hu" for our dog, Prince, (imitating panting); "mama" or "mamama" for Mama or milk; "uuuhh" for hug, as he reaches out to us; "Yaya" for our Aunt Della, whom we call Yaya. He uses about 12 signs: milk, phone (holds hand to ear), more, please, thank you, me, music (he acts like directing a choir), guitar, want, ice cream, Mama, Daddy.

I am concerned about his lack of wanting to communicate with us. I show him something he likes, yogurt, and ask if he wants some. I know he does – he loves yogurt, and he will down a cup in a few seconds. I ask him if he wants some and then nod my head in an exaggerated way, but he doesn't imitate me. I try putting my hand on the top of his head after I ask the question, and I nod his head with my hand as I nod my own head. After doing this a few days in a row, one morning I ask him if he wants some yogurt. He puts his hand on top of his head and nods it. He is beginning to communicate! This is his way of answering affirmatively, until he realizes about a month later, he can nod without placing his hand on top of his head.

Nathan is starting special education preschool. He has an IEP (Individualized Educational Plan) with very low goals. I would like to see higher goals for him, but I guess when he masters these goals, he will move on to higher ones.

We are trying to teach Nathan numbers by counting. He thinks we are sooo funny! He laughs so hard when he hears us counting. I wonder if it's because he has never heard these numbers and the sound of them is funny, or is it the rhythm and beat of how we sound when we count?

He can now go up and down the steps, and I'm teaching him to count the steps as he goes. He makes a sound as if he is counting, but he doesn't actually say the numbers. He always listens for rhythms and nods his head or claps his hands to the beat, whether it's the sound of a hammer, tapping or a song with a drum beat.

I made a list of things he does, things he likes, things he loves. What he loves most is for all four of us, his immediate family members, to be together in the same room. Whenever we go to a restaurant, Nathan is very distracted by the other people, to the point where, if he can see anyone besides us, he won't eat. He watches the other people, and we must repeatedly turn his focus to his plate and his food. If one of us leaves the table to go to the restroom or for any other reason, he turns to watch for us until we return to the table, unsatisfied until all four of us are together again. In an unfamiliar setting, he wants all of his familiar people to stay with him.

Nathan has started to say "Yeah!" He says it when asked if he wants something, but he also he uses it as the answer to every question. I don't think he realizes the meaning. Daddy begins to call him 'Yes Man.' Nathan has never said, "No," or answered any other way.

Finally, one evening just before Christmas, during dinner, he verbally responds when I ask if he wants more! He answers, "Mo," and watches me expectantly as I serve him more food. I am so excited! Nathan responds with an answer!

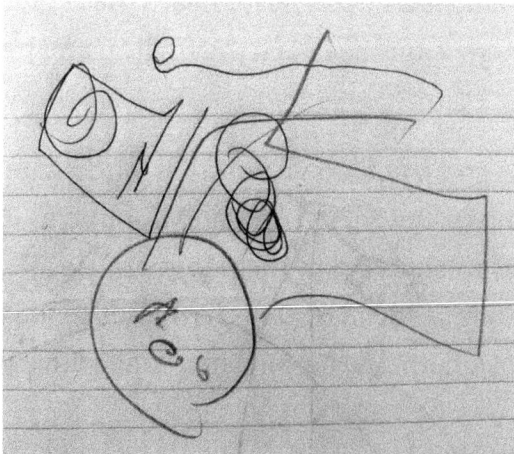

In order to motivate Nathan to do things, such as get up, get his coat, go to the kitchen, go to the bathroom on his own, I make up songs with instructions. I have been singing to him all his life, and he appreciates my musical efforts. He smiles and claps for my songs, and then does what I am asking him to do. He makes me feel like I am the best entertainer in the world. He is a great audience!

I have been trying to teach Nathan to jump off a very low stool, but he won't do it. He is always very cautious with his steps, his feet. I show him how to jump down, but no matter how many times he practices, he just steps off the stool and then does a little jump with both feet after he is on the ground.

Four

Nathan loves people and he loves to hug! He must've inherited that from his daddy, who is a real hugger. Nathan wants to hug everyone. When he walks, he wants to hold someone's hand. He is such a loving boy.

Nathan is 4 now and I discover quite by accident that he is likes musicals! I am changing channels on the TV and "Music Man" is playing, right at the part where the women are singing, "pick-a-little, talk-a-little, cheep-cheep-cheep," and Nathan is delighted! He is fascinated! He stops what he is doing to watch with all of his attention focused on the program. I have not watched many musicals, but I am excited that Nathan is showing such an interest. I keep the TV on that channel until the end of the movie, and Nathan is thrilled. During the movie, he goes to the mirror, and with one eye on the TV, he imitates the Music Man's every move. (By the way, Nathan is a great imitator, and he will imitate the gestures and hand movements of anyone who is speaking, especially his daddy, who uses his hands extensively when he is talking.)

I begin collecting videotapes of all the musicals I can find at the used tape store. Most of these productions I have never seen before, but Nathan wants to watch them over and over, so I, in my 40s, become a fan of all the famous musicals. We watch one together almost every night before bedtime, until he falls asleep. He loves to watch them over and over. Each time we get a new musical, he watches it many times to get to know it. He doesn't sing, but he learns the songs, he makes movements along with the main characters, and when we have one playing during the day, he silently performs along with the cast, while watching himself in the mirror.

One summer Sunday, we are out in front of the church just after service with lots of kids. Nathan is delighted to be around all the children. He is looking from one to the other, trying to get their attention. By now, they know and like Nathan, but he is mostly excluded from what they do, mainly for two reasons: he doesn't know how to do whatever they are doing, or they don't really think to include him. He doesn't mind. He is still content, and at this moment, he is very excited, jumping up and down with excitement.

We are all standing on the sidewalk, the kids laughing and joking, when a large truck comes barreling down the wrong side of the street, extremely close to the side where we are standing. Suddenly, Nathan jumps out into the street, right in the path of the truck. I leap behind him, grab his coat, and yank him back to safety, just in time. The driver, still speeding, takes a second to shake his fist at Nathan. I am so angry at him, the driver, for driving so fast on this street without slowing down when approaching a group of children on the side of the road, but my anger is tempered with the relief that Nathan is okay. How many times have I told Nathan to not go into the street without holding someone's hand? In the thrill of the moment, this instruction was not in his mind. I say a prayer of thanks and look around to see that no one else has even noticed Nathan's near-accident. His care and safety are up to me, up to us, his parents.

One night, in the middle of the night, his sister wakes me up. "Do you know what Nathan was doing?" she asks. My mind races to possible dangers, but she laughs, calming my fears.

"I was asleep, and I heard these gremlin noises outside my room. I turned on the light, and Nathan was sitting in the hallway with the ice cream and a spoon, eating from the carton, watching himself in the hallway mirror and making weird noises, like a gremlin talking. He must have already eaten enough, because he willingly gave me the carton when I went over to him. He let me put him back in bed without protesting. But he was making these weird sounds he's never made before!"

Five

At Nathan's checkup, we ask his doctor if anything is wrong with Nathan. He is 5 years old and barely talking. He is to start special education kindergarten in the fall, but what is his diagnosis? His doctor tells us, "Nathan is Nathan. He is not like anyone else. He is happy and physically thriving – we have no reason to put a label on him." He says Nathan is developmentally delayed in the autistic spectrum. Physically, he is developing completely normally, still a little taller and thinner than most boys his age.

One evening I tell Nathan, as he is sitting on the edge of his bed, "I wish I knew what is going on inside your head." He looks right at me and answers with a string of noises I have never heard him make before. I wonder if these are actual sounds he hears in his head, or this is his best way of answering me without using words. He looks at me as if he is expecting a response, and, for once, I don't have one for him. I smile at him with fascination and satisfaction, since he did, in his own way, answer my question.

I tell my mom about Nathan's love for musicals, and she buys season tickets for all of us to attend live Broadway shows when they come to her town. The first one we see is "The Sound of Music." Nathan is beyond thrilled to be right there, in the theater, with the actors and the live orchestra. He is the most enthusiastic person in the audience, although he is well-behaved. As I glance around at the mostly older people around us, I notice they are smiling at Nathan's excitement. This fun activity with Grandma Dixie will continue for years to come.

He has been in kindergarten for a couple of months, and his very sweet teacher tells us he has no interest in learning. He acts like he is being entertained and he is very good at watching and imitating her and the other adults. He doesn't really want to interact with the other kids or play games with them. He has pays no attention to numbers or colors; he's not grasping their concepts. We discover this at home, too, no matter what we try. I point to an object and ask him, "What color is this?" For everything, he answers, "gwee-yellow." He is interested in the rhythm and cadence of our speech, but numbers and the names of colors have no meaning to him. His teacher indicates that although Nathan doesn't seem to be learning anything academically, he is well-behaved in class and doesn't talk at school. He draws with either hand, and his teacher suggests that we get him to focus with one hand or the other, so he can train one hand and refine his writing skills.

His teacher tells us Nathan's biggest accomplishment is that he is the best eater in class. He is the only student to always use his fork while eating AND eat all of his lunch every day. On days when the boy who sits next to him is not there, Nathan grabs his fork and uses two forks to eat.

I am sure Nathan is learning, even though his progress is not obvious at school. At home, I give him a test of another kind. I gather all of his videotapes of musicals – he has 24 now – and I spread them out on his bed. He is very interested in what I am doing, and he watches my every move. I look over all the covers and I ask Nathan, "Which movie is this?" He looks at me expectantly.

I sing a phrase, "Whenever I feel afraid, I hold my head erect," from "I Whistle a Happy Tune" from "The King and I," and Nathan immediately grabs the correct cover and points to the lady who sings the song. I sing just three words, "So long, farewell," from "The Sound of Music" and he grabs the cover before I can get to the next line. I snap my fingers 4 times and he points to the cover for "West Side Story" – I don't even have to sing a line and he knows which musical it is. I sing, "O what a beautiful morning," and he points to "Oklahoma." I sing, "I'm gonna wash that man right out of my hair," and he points to "South Pacific." I sing, "You got trouble," and he points to "Music Man," before I can sing, "right here in River City." I go on to sing just one line from one song on each movie, and he gets them all right! He can match each song to the correct movie by the videotape covers! He doesn't miss one, even with my renditions, no matter which song I sing, or who was the original singer!

I share this test of his knowledge of musicals with his kindergarten teacher the next time we have a conference with her, and she is very impressed, although she does not see how that has an impact on his learning at school. For me, it is a fantastic breakthrough, letting me know that Nathan is learning, he has great memory, and he is able to connect even my versions of famous songs with the original movies.

Six

At the end of kindergarten, Nathan has not made much academic progress: he can't read or identify letters or numbers or colors. His vocabulary is extremely limited: he still says only a few words. I feel that he needs more time to learn these beginning skills. During his IEP meeting at the end of the year, I ask if he can repeat kindergarten, so he has another chance to learn the alphabet, numbers and colors. If he can go over it again in a classroom setting, I think he will be successful, because things will start to fall into place in his brain. He needs lots of repetition. The school principal who is in the meeting tells us that because of the new "No Child Left Behind" requirement, students are not allowed to repeat a grade, but not to worry – when he is in high school, he can repeat his senior year until he turns 21. I am very disappointed. Since he is already behind, every year as the class moves ahead, Nathan will not be able to catch up. Nathan will move into first grade without mastering any kindergarten skills (except he does eat all of his lunch and always uses his fork).

(SIDE NOTE: Years later, I learned that this was not the intent of "No Child Left Behind," and, as a parent, I could have demanded that Nathan repeat kindergarten. But I learned this too late. Parents, you know what is best for your own child. Ask for it.)

During the summer after kindergarten, Nathan learns to sign "no," although his version is a bit modified from the standard sign language version. He is not always Yes Man now. Even though he doesn't say "no" out loud, almost every time we ask him a question, he responds by signing, "No."

Nathan lost his first tooth! We don't know where it is.

I am trying my best to understand Nathan. He wants a routine, but, more than that, I think he wants to know what is going on, what is coming up next. The calendar makes no sense to him, which makes it hard for us to convey to him what is happening when. I know they use schedules at school, but to a person who can't read, what good are they?

And it's not just that he can't read – he refuses to look at books. We have many children's books, and he won't look at them, although he does enjoy listening to me read when the words have a rhythm, like Dr. Suess books do. When I am reading to him, he bobs his head to the rhythm of my voice. He likes the way I use different voices for different characters in the book, and he watches me as I am reading. I have a hard time getting him to look at the pictures in the book. I point to the pictures and, while he is still looking at me, he taps his finger on the book without looking at it. He disregards cartoons and comics. He is, however, very interested in photos, especially of his family and people he knows.

I work in a school library and have been checking out children's books to read to him for years, but he has no interest in any of them. One day, a co-worker suggests I take him a book with photos instead of drawings. I find a book, "A Moose for Jessica," about a moose that seems to fall in love with a cow. This book has no drawings, no illustrations, but it has photos on every page. I am hopeful that Nathan will at least look at the photos.

He loves it! He is very attentive when I show it to him! He keeps turning the pages back and forth to look at the photos, pointing at the moose and the cow. I read it to him over and over, and he keeps pointing at the moose and the cow, saying, very dragged out, "mooooooo" and "coooowww." Finally, I feel like I have made a breakthrough! A drawing of a mouse with a cookie has no significance to him, because the drawings don't, in his mind, represent a mouse and a cookie. Photographs make sense to him. He can recognize a moose and a cow in photos.

Nathan still has only a few words he uses, and many of his words, only I can understand. I contact our health insurance company to request speech/language therapy services for him. They reject the request on the grounds that they don't provide for therapy services for a person with a 'speech delay.' I call their phone number and explain to them that our son, at 6 years old, only uses about 25 words; this is more than just a speech delay. He is not talking. They tell me they are sorry, they can't help me. I write a letter explaining the situation: a 6-year-old who basically can't talk, can they please reconsider our request? The insurance company does not respond. I write a second letter, and again, they do not respond.

Nathan is in the first grade, and we love his new teacher. He has a one-on-one aide, a girl he adores, and he is obedient to her. He mostly behaves at school, but he does need lots of prompting when it's time to change activities. (We have noticed this at home. He has a hard time with transitions.) He also needs reminders to not

hit at or kick at other kids. (I'm not making excuses for him, but I think his lack of communication skills leaves him with few options when he wants to get the attention of others.) He listens to adults and he will probably have a one-on-one aide for his entire school career, unless he miraculously starts behaving without repeated prompting, reminders and directions.

One day I get a call while I am at work that Nathan had an accident at school! The school nurse thinks he needs stitches! I rush over to his school and Nathan is sitting calmly in the office waiting for me, very happy to see me. He has a large bandage on his forehead, with blood soaking through it. "Mama! Mama!" he says, coming to hug me. The teacher is so worried, so apologetic, as she explains that Nathan got a new aide today, and when the students were lining up for lunch, Nathan just jumped out of line and fell and hit his head on a desk. The nurse and his teacher tell me that he didn't cry or acknowledge pain in any way. The nurse gives me another large bandage, since the one he has will soon need to be replaced. Now he is so happy to be leaving school with me.

His school is just a few blocks from the urgency care clinic, so I take Nathan there instead of clear across town to his doctor. When I check him in, the receptionist assesses his wound then tells us we have to wait about an hour. The waiting room is empty, but in a minute two people are brought in who apparently stabbed each other, from what I overhear.

I change the bandage on Nathan's head, and since he has missed his lunch, I take him next door to Dairy Queen, where he enjoys a milkshake. We go back to the clinic and when we are finally taken to a room, they strap Nathan to the bed with Velcro straps. (I think how handy that might be at home, since, at times, he does get up during the night and wander around the house.)

Nathan does not complain or make a sound while the doctor is examining him, but he struggles a couple of times against the straps, trying to sit up. The cut is right in the middle of his forehead, about an inch long, near his hair line. The doctor tells me Nathan needs a few stitches.

As the doctor is working on him and I am holding Nathan's hand (but not looking at his forehead since I can't stand to see blood, much less a needle going into my baby's forehead), Nathan doesn't complain or cry. At one point, Nathan says, "Ow." That is the extent of his reaction to this pain.

He doesn't seem to feel or react to the pain of splitting open his forehead. Yet, on the other hand, he can't stand the feeling of a tag in his shirt. If his shirt or pajamas have a tag at the back of his neck, when he is lying down for a nap or at bedtime, he reaches back and rips it out. Many of his shirts and pajama tops need to be repaired after he pulls out the tags. One day, I take him for a walk and when we get home, I discover a large rock in his shoe! He doesn't seem to notice the big pains, but those little tags are a real irritation to him.

During the summer, I take Nathan to the 90th birthday party of one of the members of our church. We arrive at the party, and about 10 other people are there: a few adults and a few kids we know from church. We are in the back yard and the owner of the house has an in-ground swimming pool. Some of the kids are in the pool, the little ones sitting on the steps in the shallow end so just their feet are in the water. Nathan loves water! He wants to join them. I take off his shoes and shirt and tell him to sit beside the little boys on the step. He sits and splashes with the others, laughing while I watch them.

The birthday boy is in the house, and another lady has secretly brought a cake (another thing Nathan really loves) to surprise him. She asks me how many candles she should put on the cake for a 90-year-old. I turn my back on the pool and walk over to see the cake.

I am almost to the table where the cake is, when suddenly one of the boys shouts, "Mrs. Pride! Nathan—" and I turn to see Nathan's head bobbing in the water, as his body glides towards the deep end of the pool, about 25 feet away from me. (Did I mention that the pool has a very steep slope at the bottom? No, I didn't know either.) In that instant, before the boy finishes his sentence, I race over to the pool, jump into the water, and pull Nathan to safety in the shallow end. The boy is apologizing, saying Nathan just launched himself into the water and tried to go where the other boy was swimming, in the deep end. I get Nathan out of the pool as he is coughing up water, and I take him inside to the bathroom. I dry us off and wrap us up in towels. I am scared for what could have happened, mad at myself for turning away from Nathan when he was in the pool, even though he was sitting on the steps with the other kids in the shallow end. It only took a couple of seconds for him to make his move and be in danger.

When we come out to the yard, everyone is pretty much back to normal. My heart is still racing, and I remind myself that Nathan must always be supervised; he can't be trusted to do anything on his own, since he doesn't understand about safety and danger.

Suddenly I wonder, where are my sandals? They must be at the bottom of the pool. Nope, there they are, about 4 feet apart, leading into the pool. I must've jumped out of them as I jumped into the pool. We join the others and Nathan gets his piece of cake and mine too – I am too worked up to eat right now.

Seven

Now Nathan is 7 years old and my husband and I take him to a family sign language immersion weekend (no voice allowed) where we can all learn more about communicating in sign. Participants are separated into levels of sign language knowledge. Nathan refuses to go with the children beginners without me, so I go to his classes with him. My husband goes to the adult beginner class. At lunch time, Nathan and I arrive at the cafeteria with his class before the other classes arrive, and Nathan begins to get anxious that Daddy isn't here. He keeps signing, "Daddy. Daddy. Daddy." I can't think of how to tell him that Daddy will soon be here, since we are not allowed to use our voices. One of the Deaf teachers comes over to our table and Nathan signs to her, "Daddy." She teaches him the sign for "wait," and somehow, he understands the concept! To this day, when something isn't happening right now, Nathan will sign and say, "Waaaait," knowing that it will soon come to pass.

Nathan begins to say "Hi," to everyone. Nathan, like his daddy, loves people, loves everyone, so I attempt to teach Nathan about not talking to strangers. I tell him, "Just say 'Hi,' and that's all." After this, when we meet people in the store or anywhere we go, Nathan says, "Hi." The person generally responds with "Hi," and Nathan again says, "Hi." He will continue saying "Hi," until I stop him. I think about how he is being obedient, saying "Hi," and that's all. (Or is it because he doesn't know the next words to use in conversation?)

During the summer after first grade, Nathan begins to say "No." He says it while he is signing, "no," his automatic response to everything. I think about 2-year-olds who go through a phase of saying, "no," and I hope this will be a similar phase, though much delayed, which won't last long.

Nathan loves creating art on the computer. We have an art program, "Kid Pix," he has been using for about three years, and he has created hundreds of pictures with it. He likes the sounds it makes as well as the designs; different tools make different sounds, so as he creates, he has an auditory experience as well as a visual experience. One of his favorite poses: he loves to lie on his side on the floor manipulating the mouse on his leg, watching the screen, as he creates.

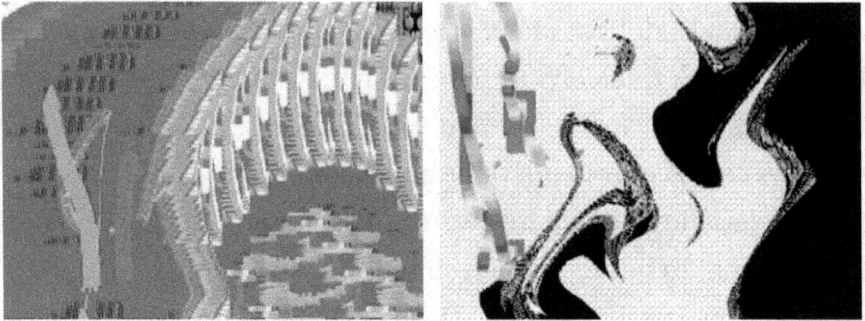

Kid Pix creations by Nathan

Eight

When Nathan is 8, we are given a new puppy and Nathan loves her. He has always loved our big dog, Prince, who is so patient with Nathan, and he loves our large, mellow, older cat, Punkin, who is fine with Nathan. We are at first concerned about having this new puppy around Nathan. However, we soon discover that the puppy can take care of herself and she lets Nathan pet her, hold her and feed her. We name the puppy Sheba, a name Nathan can pronounce; but sometimes he forgets her name. (He does that with words sometimes, forgets them.) He calls her 'Pizza,' 'Beeza,' or 'Pucky.' So, I make up a name sign for her, S-B near my mouth. Now when I ask him, "What is the puppy's name?" he looks at me, waiting for me to tell him. When I show her name sign, he remembers and says, "Sheba."

In the spring when Nathan is 8 years old, the school district tells us they need a more specific label on him for next fall. 'Pervasive Developmental Delay in the Autistic Spectrum' isn't enough for them. The district refers us to a specialist in Portland, Oregon, and we spend several hours with him, answering pages and pages of questions as he observes Nathan interacting with us. At the end of the evaluation, the specialist gives us a few clues about what is going on in Nathan's mind.

A. Nathan's brain works differently from ours. His mind takes more time to process information than ours. This is why he has a delayed reaction to our questions and directions. He is not being disobedient.

B. Nathan's senses, especially hearing and sight, are heightened, more sensitive to stimuli than ours, and his senses are not isolated from each other. A loud sound can trigger sensations of bright lights or a feeling of pain.

C. Nathan's hearing is excellent, yet it is not focused – this is why he 'listens around the house.' He has a hard time focusing on the sounds right in front of him. We have trained our brains to filter out irrelevant sounds, but he has to learn how to do that.

D. Nathan is very happy, very satisfied with his life and his family. The specialist told us he rarely sees children who are as happy as Nathan. He doesn't see anything in Nathan that is 'broken' and needs to be fixed.

The specialist gives the official diagnosis of 'Intellectually Disabled in the Autistic Spectrum.' He discusses what it means for a child to be on the autistic spectrum, that each child is at a different point. A few of his behaviors, such as his unfocused super-hearing and his tendency to take things literally are indicators that Nathan is on the spectrum; even though many of his behaviors, such as hugging and looking me in the eye are not considered to be behaviors of persons on the spectrum. The doctor tells us not to focus on the diagnosis, but on who Nathan is and what he can do.

When we get home from the appointment, I ask God to help me to understand Nathan better. I start working on Clue C, the one that will be the easiest for me to experience: I begin to pay attention to sounds outside our immediate room, trying to listen as Nathan listens. I consciously make myself aware of other sounds in the room, in the rest of the house, and outside the house.

I know he listens to us talking, wherever we are, from his room. If we mention his sister, who is now away at college, he comes from his room and says her name, over and over. If we are in the kitchen and we discuss an upcoming trip to visit a relative, he will later say that relative's name, again and again, until we explain when we are going to see him/her again. We know Nathan hears us talking in the other room, no matter where we are in the house. I force my ears to pay attention all other sounds – airplanes flying over, cars driving by or people shouting outside, music playing in another room – besides only focusing on the important sounds and conversation within the room where I am.

On Sunday, are getting ready to go to church. We are standing at the top of the staircase, on the landing, and my husband tells Nathan to go and get his coat from his room. Nathan stands still, looks straight ahead, and responds, "Beee-beee-beee." Daddy says, "Not be-be-be! I told you to go get your coat!" I quickly make the leap to what Nathan is hearing outside of our immediate focus: a truck outside is backing up and beeping! "Yes, Nathan, a truck is backing up. But you need to do what Daddy said and go get your coat." As soon as I acknowledge that I know what he hears, he goes and gets his coat.

(SIDE NOTE: When Nathan was small enough to sit in the grocery basket, every time I would back up the basket in the store, he would say, "Beee-beee-beee." He knew a vehicle backing up made a beeping sound. This gave me the hint of what he was hearing now.)

Over the next few days, I notice Nathan marking the beat to a clock ticking, the signal light blinking, a woodpecker in one of our trees, a neighbor beating on a drum. He imitates the sounds of the dog snoring, the refrigerator and lamp humming. Nathan knows that I know what he is hearing! He asks me, "What's that?" ("Wussat?") when he hears the furnace rumbling, a plane flying over, a noisy car driving by, a neighbor's dog barking. He is asking me, in his own way, if I am aware of these other sounds outside our normal range of focus, letting me know that he does hear something that is not being mentioned.

A few days later, the first concept (Clue A) that the doctor told us about Nathan's mind needing processing time clicks in my mind when I see a person signing on a program on TV. I know Sign Language, but my native language is English. When someone is communicating in Sign Language, I don't get it right away. My mind has to process it. When someone signs to me, "Get the books from the table and give them to me," I don't respond immediately because I have to process the signs into words: **books on table, give to me.** It might take just a couple of seconds, but I now become aware of this time lag as my mind is processing the information. This is what is happening with Nathan! His brain is processing what we tell him, and it takes a few seconds for him to get it! My husband and I need to be patient with him and realize that his mind doesn't automatically understand the words we say; it needs time to process the words before he can react.

This is a huge breakthrough in my understanding of Nathan's mind. I explain it to my husband, but since he has not learned any other languages, this doesn't make as much sense to him; but I feel like I get it. I begin to use the phrase "processing time" to help my husband remember why Nathan doesn't instantly respond to a question or direction, and by the time I say it, Nathan's mind has the bit of time it needs to process the information, and he responds. It's not a long time, only a few seconds; it's just longer than we are used to. When we speak to people, we expect immediate results, but we, as parents of Nathan, must be patient with him just a few seconds longer. Ask me a question in Sign Language and I will review it, translate it, figure out what you mean; not immediately, but after a few seconds of processing time, and then I will react or respond.

The second concept, Clue B, Nathan's senses overlapping or not being isolated from each other, is shown to me by God a couple of days later. This might happen to a lot of people, and there is probably a name for it, but at a time when I experience my senses 'overlap' I feel like I have a better understanding of Nathan and his sensory perception. I am in bed, just about to fall asleep, and outside is a very loud sound like a gunshot. I hear it, yes, but I also see it and I feel it. In this state between wake and sleep, I see a bright white-blue burst like a huge firework behind my eyelids, and a pain shoots through my body at the same instant as I hear the sound. (No, I have not actually been shot.) The sound has triggered both a sight and a feeling in my body – two of my other senses are connected to my hearing of this loud sound.

I sit up in bed and think of Nathan, how he says, "Ow!" when he hears a loud sound – how the auditory stimulus crosses over to his sense of feel and it hurts him for an instant. This is what the doctor meant! His senses are not isolated from each other and their reactions overlap. I get it now!

A friend of mine is in an Elvis tribute band. We take Nathan to see the band play. Nathan is fascinated with Elvis! He is captivated during the performance, watching the guitarists and especially the Elvis character when he sings. When we get home afterwards, Nathan finds an Elvis movie among his videos and watches it. He plays it over and over during the next few days. I decide to buy more Elvis movies for him.

A coworker mentions a horse therapy farm just out of town, and we take Nathan to try it. He won't get on a horse unless I do it first. I am afraid of horses and I don't like being up that high - but I get on the extremely docile horse and ride around the yard once, with my husband and Nathan walking alongside. Then Nathan follows my example and he rides on the horse! He likes it! We take him back a few times during the summer. He tolerates the experience, but his favorite part is when we get finished and go get ice cream.

In the fall after Nathan starts third grade, Nathan communicates with me! He speaks to me on his own, not a reaction to a question or something we said. We are standing outside, waiting for his school bus on a drizzly, dreary morning, and he looks at me and says, "Cold." I answer him, trying to contain my excitement at this first Nathan-initiated conversation and say, "Yes! Yes, you are right! It is cold out here!" I hug him close to me, to warm us both, and in celebration of this breakthrough he has made.

Two nights later, he communicates again at the dinner table! We are eating dinner, and he points to the food on his plate and says, "Good." Tears fill my eyes over a seemingly simple thing, one word, which is a huge milestone to me. Yes, it's wonderful when a family member tells you the dinner you made is good, but now Nathan is speaking his own mind, not only reacting to something that was said to him!

The next day, he and I are taking a walk and my nose starts to run. I ask Nathan, "Do you have a Kleenex in your pocket?" He stops walking and checks both of his pockets, then he tells me, "All gone." I am over-the-moon excited that Nathan has begun to use his words to communicate! He has correctly answered a question I asked him!

Nathan is in the last quarter of third grade when we have his annual IEP conference with his teacher, whom he had all through the second grade as well. She is disappointed at his lack of progress. She says he seems to be paying attention to her and to his one-on-one aide, but he is not doing his class work and does not seem at all interested in reading, the alphabet, numbers or colors. (We have heard this before.) She goes over his IEP with us again and she does not change any of his goals. She says he will continue to work on his same goals as he has had since first grade.

Just as we are finishing the conference and getting ready to leave, she asks, "What do you do when you tell Nathan to do something and he just laughs at you? Whenever I tell him to do anything, he just laughs and laughs at me." My husband and I tell her that he never does that with us. She says he has been laughing at her every time she talks to him, ever since he joined her class at the beginning of second grade. (Why hasn't she told us this before?)

Later that evening, as I am reviewing in my mind what his teacher told us in the conference, I hear her question in my mind and it hits me: Nathan thinks she has a funny voice, and he is laughing at the sound of her voice! Her high-pitched, whiny voice sounds the same as one of the funny voices I use when I am reading to him and trying to get him interested in a book! I realize that Nathan will never take her voice seriously. The next day I call the Special Education office and ask if Nathan can be transferred to another class or school. I am more than a little angry with the teacher that she has not mentioned this behavior before. Nathan has lost nearly two years of learning at school while he thought he was merely being entertained by a teacher using a funny voice to make him laugh!

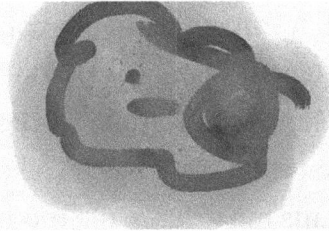

Nine

Ever since Nathan was a baby, I have been brushing his teeth every night. Yes, he tries to brush them, but he mostly does only one area, the lower right quadrant (or left, when he uses his left hand) so I help him finish up by brushing the rest of his teeth. In order to help him stay focused and not pull away from me, I sing a song while I am brushing, one of the songs I make up specifically for teeth-brushing. Daddy helps Nathan brush his teeth every morning. I emphasize the importance of keeping his teeth clean and healthy, especially since he loves ice cream so much. I don't want him to feel pain when he eats ice cream due to teeth problems.

We, either my husband or I, have taken Nathan to the dentist every year, and he has never had a cavity or any problems. The difficulty is getting him to open his mouth for the exam, but with much coaxing and everyone else in the room opening our mouths, he will eventually open for the dentist.

I take Nathan to the dentist at age 9 for his regular checkup and he has a new dentist, a female, with a very long and unusual name. She tells us Nathan has six cavities! I am shocked! How can he suddenly have so many cavities? She tells us this is common in children, although in our family it is not common. (Our daughter has never had a cavity and I have had only three in my life.) The dentist tells us that because of Nathan's disability and inability to sit still while in the dental chair, he will need to be anesthetized for the procedure and they can't do it in the office. We need to take him to a special dentist office at the children's hospital in Portland.

We receive approval from our insurance company, and I notice the same unusual dentist's name as the one will be doing the fillings at the hospital. I'm glad – Nathan will be more comfortable during the procedure since he knows her. I take Nathan to the appointment. An aide wants me to leave the room, but Nathan panics and keeps trying to get out of the bed, so I am allowed to stay in the room with him. I softly sing songs to coax Nathan to stay in the bed. He really wants to get up. I keep him entertained for the next 45 minutes while we wait.

A male doctor comes into the room, telling us he will be taking care of Nathan, and I notice his name tag. He has the same long, unusual last name as Nathan's dentist. I make a remark about this, and he looks at me oddly, pauses (he didn't know I would notice?), and tells me that his wife was the one who wrote the referral.

Nathan is given the anesthetic and the dentist works quickly. I can't see exactly what he is doing from the chair where I am sitting, but he is finished in less than 10 minutes. The aide wheels the bed out to a recovery room, tells me Nathan will be asleep for at least another 45 minutes and should stay lying down for a minimum of 15 minutes after that. He tells me to call for him when Nathan wakes up and he will bring him a popsicle. He gives me a pile of paperwork to take with me, and says we can leave the hospital in an hour, after Nathan wakes up, as soon as he feels like walking. I sit down beside the bed with a book I'm planning to read.

Nathan wakes up the minute the aide leaves the room and tries to get up. (What happened to 45 minutes?) The aide hears him and brings a popsicle. Nathan is not interested and struggles to sit up. I hold him down, telling him he needs to rest, but he fights me, sits up, and swings his legs down onto the floor. He is too strong for me to hold him down. I tell him he needs to stay in the bed, but he refuses. I check the clock: we arrived at the hospital less than an hour ago. I make him sit in the chair for about a minute, but he is insistent that we must leave the room. I am right beside him, holding him, in case he loses his balance, and he forcefully pulls me to the door, down the hall to the elevator. He is not staying in that place a minute longer. Nathan stays awake during our 40-minute drive home. By the time we get home, Nathan is back to himself again, and not sleepy at all.

At home, the next time I brush Nathan's teeth, I try to see his six new fillings. I ask him to open his mouth wide (he has a big mouth; he can open it very wide) and I can only see one filling. I wonder where the other five fillings are, figuring they must be between teeth, or where? I can't see them.

A week later, we receive the bill for Nathan's 6 fillings, which is over $7500. We are responsible for 10% and our insurance will pay the rest. I ponder the fact that one dentist sent Nathan to her dentist husband for a procedure that took less than 10 minutes and the doctor / hospital earned $7500+, and I can't even find five of the brand new fillings.

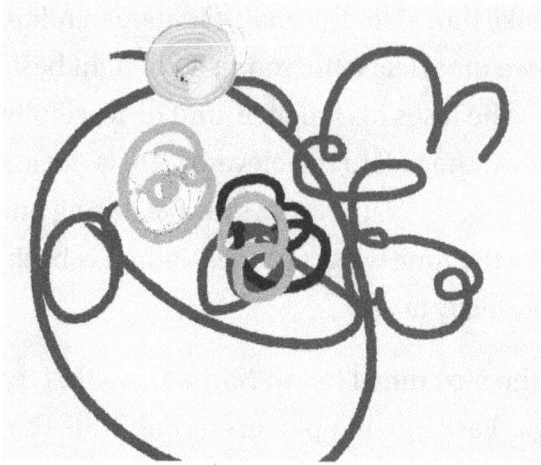

Ten

Nathan has so much empathy for others. If someone gets emotional and cries at church, he will do one of three things: he will take the person a tissue, he will make a sad face and hug me, or he will start to cry more loudly than the other person. He isn't doing this as an act. He is truly sad when someone is crying. His teacher says he does the same things at school when a student gets upset, although there he is more likely to give the student a tissue and try to give him or her a hug. Unfortunately, hugs are not allowed at school, so Nathan has to be satisfied giving a 'high five,' although we all know that a high five is not nearly as comforting as a hug.

I get an electric toothbrush for Nathan, and he lets me use it to brush his teeth. I hand it to him and he also uses it, although he only brushes one quadrant, no matter how many times I show him how to brush all of his teeth. He is such a good imitator; why won't he imitate the way I brush my teeth? So, he starts the brushing and I finish up, cleaning the rest of his teeth. I feel like we are making much progress with his dental hygiene. I don't want him to ever have six cavities again!

Eleven

Nathan finally will tell me if he is not feeling well! If his stomach hurts, he points to it and says, "Sick." If he has a cough and his throat hurts, he points to his neck and says, "Sick." I am so grateful for this small bit of communication from him! He is so rarely sick that he doesn't need to tell us very often, but now he does have a way to tell us if something hurts.

Every night when Nathan gets in bed, he says, "Bus." This is his way of asking what is happening tomorrow: will he be riding the bus to school? Using the calendar still makes no sense to him, even though I put an X in the days as they pass and draw a picture of what will be happening on specific days.

Twelve

Nathan is 12 when we move to the city where my mom and my brother live. Nathan is so excited! We can see Grandma Dixie and Uncle Dale every week instead of just a few times a year.

Now Nathan has a collection of Halloween costumes, which he uses as props while watching his favorite musicals. He puts on his pirate vest and hat while watching "Peter Pan" or "Pirates of Penzance" (one of his very favorites), his cowboy hat when he watches Elvis Western movies, his police hat and shirt with a badge during "West Side Story."

Nathan often talks in his sleep. From our bedroom across the hall, I can hear him saying, "Bus," "Mama," Daddy," "Cake," "Nope," "Okay," "I want ice cream, please." One night when he is talking, I go into his room to check to see if he is asleep, and he is. He lifts his arm as if he is checking his watch (he loves to wear a watch, yet he can't tell time, has no concept of time) and then he salutes, all while he is sound asleep.

He really loves Elvis! Nathan listens to him singing and makes the moves right along with him, watching himself in the mirror. For Halloween, he wants to dress like Elvis, so I find the perfect outfit, white pants and shirt, and I sew on gold trim. I add a fancy gold belt and a sequined scarf. On Halloween, he looks and acts just like Elvis. He doesn't care about trick-or-treating, he just loves to dress up like Elvis and watch himself perform in the mirror. And an excellent Elvis he makes!

Nathan is overjoyed when a family with five children starts coming to our church! I teach the Sunday School class, so he gets to spend time with them. All week long, every week, he says their names, counting them on his fingers, nodding his head when he says each one. He especially likes the girl who is near his age.

We decide to get a mini iPad for Nathan, and he takes to it immediately. I load up some children's apps and books, and he goes through each of them. He especially loves the ones with sounds and the drawing apps. Whereas I have always struggled to get him to even look at a regular book, he will spend hours looking at electronic books, if we let him.

One thing, I wish I could lock the settings. After he has it for just one week, he hands it to me and I am frustrated to see that he has changed the main language to Korean. Changing it back to English takes quite a bit of tech research.

Thirteen

We cannot ever leave Nathan at home alone, and I often take him shopping with me. We go to the grocery store and now he is way too big to ride in the basket. I need to keep him entertained, interested, so he will stay with me. I have him push the basket, giving him something to do. I am pointing out foods that he likes, yogurt and cheese and he suddenly bolts away from me. He is gone, out of my sight! I quickly follow him towards the ice cream aisle, but he is already gone. I walk as fast as I can, up and down aisles, looking left and right, and I can't find him. I begin to panic. He wouldn't leave the store without me, would he? I am now running back and forth, combing the store. I hear my name paged over the intercom system, calling me to go to check stand number 6. When I get there, I find Nathan, holding the arm of a friend of mine whom he knows. Whew! She tells me he ran over to her, but she couldn't find me.

A couple months later, during another trip to a large grocery store, this time with my husband and Nathan, I tell them I need to use the ladies' room. My husband tells he me is going to look at the tools in this area. When I come out of the restroom, my husband and Nathan are not in the area where the tools are. I start looking up and down the aisles, and I see Nathan walking with a man, holding his arm - and they are going towards the door! One of my worst nightmares: Nathan is leaving the store with a stranger! I begin to run after them, and I shout, "Nathan!" They both turn around and see me. It turns out to be a local pastor that we know, and they are looking for me. The pastor tells me that my husband decided to go to the other side of the store so the pastor took Nathan to look for me.

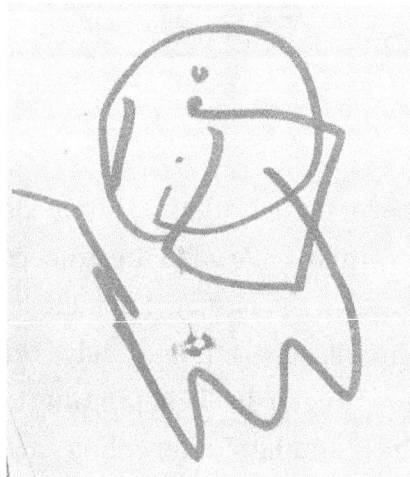

Fourteen

Nathan and I go to Costco (a very large warehouse store) to order a cake for a special occasion at church. We are not going to be in the store long since I am not going to make any purchases today, so we don't get a basket. We walk down the aisle and talk about the cake, a subject in which he is very interested. We get to the back of the store near the bakery where cakes are ordered and I fill out the order form while Nathan looks at the cakes on display, pointing to each one and saying, "Cake. Cake. Cake." As I slide the order form into the slot, suddenly Nathan takes off and turns a corner before I can stop him. I begin to run, but I don't see him down that aisle. I look back and forth, up and down every aisle, moving so quickly, but I can't find him. I check where they have the food samples, but he isn't there. I go to the front of the store, but I can't find him anywhere! I pray that he didn't leave the store!

I go to the first employee I see and explain the situation: my son has special needs, he can't say his name, he won't come to me if I call him, and he just ran away from me. She asks what he is wearing, and I tell him he has on a black jacket and plaid shirt with jeans. She gets on her radio and at this moment I realize how many people in the store are actually employees and not customers, when I see a bunch of people lift up their radios and listen. Immediately, another employee replies over the radio, "I just saw him in electronics." They find him within 30 seconds and I rush over to him, where he is playing with a computer. "Look!" he says, showing me the computer, completely unaware that I was just in full panic mode.

Thanks to the swift actions and coordination of the employees of Costco, Nathan and I are quickly reunited.

Fifteen

Shortly after Nathan turns 15, my dad (his Grandpa Joe) moves to our town. Now Nathan is soooo happy – all of his favorite family members (except his sister) live in the same town! He gets to see them more than once a week. He often says, "You-me-all of us," and I ask him, "What about it?" He answers, "Grandma Dixie." This is his way of saying he wants to go to our monthly family dinner celebration at Grandma's house, where we all get together. A couple of times each year, this also includes his sister. On those occasions, he shows her off, yet stays connected to her, as if she is his own precious jewel.

Nathan becomes a whiz at finding videos on YouTube using his iPad. He can't read, but he can find an Elvis video in a matter of seconds. My husband, Nathan and I go to the mall to look for shoes for Nathan. While we are there, we see a sign that says 'Las Vegas,' and my husband and I sing (just one line) in unison, "Viva Las Vegas!" Immediately when we get home, Nathan finds Elvis singing "Viva Las Vegas" on YouTube!

I buy a set of sonic toothbrushes for our family, since this type are supposed to clean better. Nathan hasn't had any cavities in years, and I want to keep it that way. I turn on the new toothbrush and start to lift it up toward his mouth. His hands fly to his ears as he cries out in pain, backing away from me, before the toothbrush even gets close to his mouth. He can hear the 'sonic' and it hurts his ears! No sonic toothbrush for Nathan. He will stick with the regular electric toothbrush.

Visual schedules I made

Nathan's teacher says she uses a visual schedule for Nathan, so I decide to try this idea. I get a small white board, and every night I draw 2-3 activities that Nathan will be doing the next day: a bus, some food, the church, his caregiver (who comes a few hours each week to give us a short break), the car (if we will be going somewhere in the car), the dog, if we will be taking her for a walk. I show him and tell him the plan for tomorrow, yet he still says, each night as he is getting into bed, "Bus." I review the plan in the morning, after he gets dressed for school, showing him and telling him what is happening today. After drawing and discussing his daily plans for about 3 months, Nathan still doesn't seem to understand why I am doing this. We both lose interest, but I did think a visual schedule was a good idea at the time.

Sixteen

Nathan is selected by his school Homecoming Committee to be the Duke of Homecoming! They have an assembly and present Nathan with a medal! They ask him to parade around the gym with the Homecoming Court, but he refuses to walk with them. His teacher tells us about his award and his reluctance to march around the gym.

A girl from our church agrees to go to the Homecoming Dance with Nathan! She shows me the color of her dress, golden yellow, and asks me to get Nathan a matching shirt. I find a nice gold shirt for him that perfectly matches her dress. I go to his school to buy the tickets. She and Nathan make a beautiful couple, all dressed up, Nathan wearing his suit and tie, and his Duke medal. My husband and I take the young couple out to dinner at a nice restaurant and Nathan is too excited to eat. We drop them off at the Convention Center where the dance is being held. My husband wants to stay, but we leave them to enjoy the dance with their peers. When we go back after the dance to pick them up, she tells us that Nathan was very well behaved, but he only would dance with her two times. We are so happy that she gave Nathan this opportunity; I have to hold back my tears of joy. What a blessing for Nathan. He really likes her.

The three of us, my husband, Nathan and I, go to Seattle and stay in a nice hotel downtown. Our room is on the 18th floor – the hotel has 35 floors. We enjoy the room, the view and our weekend vacation. On Saturday evening, we decide to go to the chicken restaurant across the street. The hotel has three elevators, and one isn't working. The other two have doors that close very quickly. We have to wait quite a while for the elevator, and when it arrives on our floor, people are remarking at how fast the doors shut.

We go get our meal and decide to take it back to the room to eat it. Each of us is carrying a bag of food as we step into the crowded elevator. When we arrive at the floor, I am the first one out. My husband steps out behind me and the doors quickly shut before Nathan can get out! The elevator continues its journey up, with about eight people still on it.

My husband and I have to make a very quick plan. I set my bag on a nearby table. The elevator comes back, and Nathan is not on it! He has gotten off on another floor! My husband waits to see if he comes back, perhaps on the other elevator, and he keeps pushing the button so the elevators will stop on our floor, while I go to the stairs and run up to the next floor, 19, and call for Nathan. He's not on 19. I run up to 20 and call his name. Not there. Every floor looks exactly the same! He wouldn't go into someone else's room, would he?

I run up to 21. Not there. Up to 22. Not there. 23. Not there. 24. Not there. 25. Nope. 26. Not there, either. My legs are killing me, and I am out of breath. Maybe he has returned to our floor? Hope-hope. I run back down the stairs to 18, and my husband is still waiting, watching the elevators. I tell him I am going down to the first floor, lobby, to look for Nathan. The lobby is full of people, and I look all over to see if he is among the crowds. He's not. I rush over to the desk and explain the situation. The desk clerk calls the head of security, who, thankfully, tells me that a person fitting Nathan's description is up on the 33rd floor, waiting in the hallway with a security guard. I ride the elevator up, and it stops on 18 again. I explain to my husband that I'm going up to 33, Nathan is there, before the door snaps shut.

When I arrive on Floor 33, here is Nathan, leaning against a dresser with the security guard, a young man not much older than Nathan. "Mom!" he shouts, as if he has been waiting for me to find him. Then he simply says, "Hungry." I thank the young man and take Nathan back to 18, where he is happy to be reunited with Daddy. Nathan has no problem eating the chicken dinner, but I have lost my appetite.

We must make sure, from now on, that Nathan will always exit the elevator before we do.

I take Nathan to see "The Music Man" when it's put on by our local theater group. Nathan knows this musical very well, and, as always, he is performing in his seat, along with the actors. When they get to the part where the lady points and exclaims, "It's the Wells Fargo wagon!" Nathan turns completely around in his seat, looking for the wagon to come in from the back of the theater. The audience near us breaks out chuckling.

Seventeen

Nathan and I are in the car, on our way to church. A car exactly like ours, same make, model and color, passes us in the right lane and Nathan gets very excited. He points to the car and says, "Daddy-Mama-you-me-all of us!" "Yes, Nathan, that car is like ours, isn't it?" "Yeah," he says, as he nods enthusiastically.

In the summer when Nathan is 17, we go to an all-city church service with guest speaker Senior Pastor Donnie McClurkin from Perfecting Faith Church in New York. We have someof his CDs and Nathan has seen him preaching and singing on YouTube. He imitates his every move. I try to temper his enthusiasm, but Pastor Donnie looks at us and tells me to let him praise God to the fullest extent. After the service, Nathan goes and gives him a hug.

At the beginning of December, I use the calendar to show Nathan what is happening this month. I draw a cross on Sundays, when we will go to church, a little bus on each day he will go to school, a cake on December 22, Daddy's birthday, a musical note on the days we will go caroling at nursing homes, and I write "Sister" on the day when his sister will arrive. Every day I direct his attention to the calendar as I put an X through the previous day, and we review what is happening today. I count down to the day when his sister will be here. Nathan follows along, going to the calendar more than once a day. He points and asks about his sister, and I again show him as we count down the days until she will arrive.

Finally, the day is here when she arrives, and I show Nathan on the calendar. He is so excited as we go pick her up at the airport. By now, school is out for Christmas vacation and all the other activities on the calendar have passed, so we don't talk about the calendar for the rest of the month. His sister comes, we visit family, participate in all our Christmas activities, and a week later, she goes home.

A week into January, Nathan walks over to the new calendar, points at the date in the same location as the December date when his sister arrived, and he says, "Sister." He is hoping that if he puts her name on that date, she will come again!

Eighteen

During Nathan's first senior year in high school, one day he comes home with a note from his teacher saying he fell dancing like Elvis during dance class, and he twisted his ankle. She's not sure which ankle, but she says he has been limping ever since he fell. He takes a long nap after school and in the evening, I check his ankles. I gently touch each one and ask if they hurt. He says, "No." I ask him, "Where is it sick?" He points to his right knee and says, "Right HERE." I pull up his pant leg. His knee is all swollen! I touch it and he quickly pulls it away from me. Since it is now evening, we take him to the emergency room. The X-rays show nothing is broken, so his knee is wrapped and he has physical therapy for a few weeks. After that, his knee is good as new.

Nathan and I go to see the musical "Legally Blonde" when his high school puts it on. He is especially happy to see friends performing, although he is not familiar with this show. We have a great time, and he shakes hands with the actors as we leave.

When we arrive at home, Nathan goes directly to his iPad and finds another high school performance of 'Legally Blonde' on YouTube. I am impressed! How did he find it so quickly?

Nineteen

When Nathan is 19, his dentist tells us he needs to have his wisdom teeth pulled. He says that Nathan currently has two fillings and he needs one more filling.

"Are you sure he doesn't have six fillings?" I ask.

"No, he has two fillings in his molars." (I am once again angry with his previous dentist, but it's been about ten years. What can we do?) Nathan will again be given an anesthetic and put to sleep while his teeth are pulled and his filling is added.

Recalling how Nathan responded to his previous dental experience, my husband and I decide to both go with him to this appointment. Nathan is happy while we are waiting, enjoying the toys in the waiting room. When they take him into the room for his extractions, we go with him. He is very upset and he won't lie still. They give him the anesthetic, but he doesn't go all the way under. My husband and I stay in the room and hold his arm and legs, try to calm him, while they take care of his teeth.

The minute they finish, Nathan starts to get out of the chair. They won't let him, but he keeps struggling to get up. He seems completely unaware of the pain and he really wants to leave. We are required to stay in the office for 30 minutes while he recovers, so we do our best to distract him until time to take him home.

The next day, his usually slender face has turned into a fat face with chubby cheeks. After a few days, his face returns to normal. He never complains about any pain.

Twenty

One evening when my husband is out of town and Nathan and I come home late from my mom's house, Nathan is in his room doing his Elvis thing. I am in my room getting ready for bed and I hear a heavy thump sound coming from his room. I rush in to find him lying on the floor by his bed. I ask him if he hurts, and he is anxious to get up. I help him up onto the bed, wondering how and why he fell. I ask him if anything hurts and he says no. Then I ask him, "Where is it sick?" He points to his knee and says, "Right HERE." I roll up his pant leg and I don't see anything, so I give him a couple of aspirin and put him to bed.

The next morning, his knee is all swollen. Since it is Saturday, I take him to the emergency room, once again with a knee injury due to dancing like Elvis. When I explain that he has done this same thing before a few years ago, and perhaps his knee is weakened from the earlier injury, they look up the records. This time he has injured his other knee! The doctor wraps his knee and warns him to be very careful next time he is dancing like Elvis.

Twenty-one

Nathan repeats his senior year of high school four times. He never does learn to read, still doesn't understand the concept of colors or numbers. He loves his teacher and his one-on-one aide, and he learns to do a variety of jobs around the school and in the community, jobs he can do as a partner to his aide, but not on his own. Everyone at school knows him. When we go to stores or restaurants around town, we often see someone who says, "Hi, Nathan!" He recognizes them and he asks me, "Who's that?" I tell him, "I don't know, who is it?" He just smiles at me.

Just after Nathan turns 21, he is invited to be in a YouTube video! A local dance company is producing a music video starring dancers and students with special needs, showing how they can get together and everyone can be included. We go to the recording session, and Nathan refuses to stay on the stage without Daddy - so my husband gets to be in the video too! Shortly before Nathan's graduation, the video is released and we share it with all our family and friends.

Nathan finishes high school when he is 21, and we have a graduation party for him. He is so excited! We invite his school friends, teachers, neighbors, church friends, who all celebrate with our family in our back yard. We set up a photo area and everybody has photos taken with Nathan. Nathan is thrilled that all his favorite people come to celebrate with him.

After the guests leave, his sister calls out to me, "Mom! Nathan took his sock off! His toe is all black!" I rush over and take a close look. His second toe is purple, but the black is from his sock. I clean it with rubbing alcohol, and we take Nathan to his doctor the next day.

The doctor discovers Nathan's toe has become infected from a blister. He cautions me to check his toes on a regular basis, since Nathan is not one to tell us if his toe is hurting – and this is the type of situation that can lead to amputation if not caught early. That scares me. The doctor prescribes antibiotics and Nathan's toe is back to its normal color within a week. We now check his toes nightly before he gets in bed, part of his routine, after brushing his teeth.

For years, I have been singing to Nathan our phone number in a song, in hopes that he will learn and sing it, but this is one song Nathan doesn't try to repeat. He merely bobs his head to the beat of me singing the numbers. When Nathan says his own name, most people can't understand him. After he graduates from high school, we decide he must always wear an identification bracelet with our phone number on it, since if he gets away from us, in a crowd or during an activity, he can't tell anyone who he is, who we are or what is his address or phone number. I order a very fancy silver ID bracelet that he likes to wear all the time. I tell him often, "If you can't find me or Daddy, show someone this phone number and they can call me." He says, "Okay," but we don't know if he really understands.

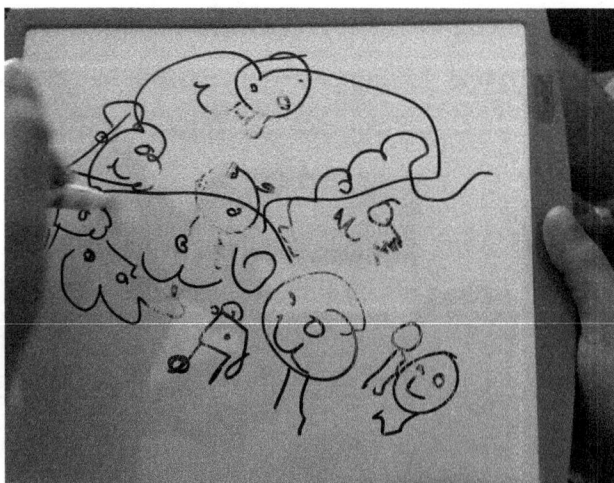

Part 2

The Poem

You might ignore me,
Yes, I am aware.
I don't act like you
But I do care.

I'm paying attention,
Everything I see.
I learn from you,
You learn about me.

I am not like others,
But then, are you?
We all have our ways,
Things we love and do.

My mind does not process
The same way as yours.
My passions are deep
Your pains are my sores.

I depend on you
Even when I don't say.
Maybe you don't understand me.
I love you anyway.

Part 3

Lessons Learned

1. Tell the People You Love that You Love Them

Nathan didn't start talking until he was almost 4 years old. He was such a happy boy, satisfied with his life. He reminded me of a story my dad told me about a boy who never said a word until he was nine years old. One evening his mother served soup for dinner and the boy said, "Soup's cold." His mother was so astonished! He was speaking for the first time! She said, "I didn't know you could talk! Why didn't you say anything before?" He replied, "Up until now, everything was fine."

When he was two, three and four, we asked Nathan's doctor why he wasn't talking, and he told us, "Nathan is Nathan. He is happy and you shouldn't worry about him not talking as early as other children. He is just being Nathan."

Nathan wanted to be around us, and he wanted our approval. He observed us and imitated our movements and gestures – but not our speech. At age four, he had a very limited spoken vocabulary, in addition to some signs.

The first phrase Nathan learned to say was "I love you." He was five years old, and not speaking much. Just as he was starting kindergarten, his sister began to say to him, very slowly, over and over, "I love you," so he could hear each word easily and distinctly. She signed it at the same time, pointing to herself while saying "I," then crossing her arms across her chest as she said, "love," then pointing to him while saying "you."

After Nathan heard her say the phrase about twenty times, he began to imitate her. He pointed to himself and said, "Ahhhhh," crossed his arms and said, "laaaah," and pointed to her and said, "you." It was a long and drawn-out phrase, but he began to say it often to us, his family members, and to his friends at school – although his teacher thought he was trying to say, "I like you," which was more appropriate for school. (Since he was already in trouble for trying to hug his classmates and teachers, I didn't let on that he was really saying, "I love you," since that also was not allowed at school.)

At this point, he had no other phrases to use, and he began to speak this phrase more quickly as he got more practice with it. He told each of us, "I love you," every time we came in contact with him, whether we had been apart all day or just in different rooms for a short time. We were so happy to hear him speaking and telling us often that he loved us.

On a daily basis, Nathan mentioned the names of his family members, his sister, Grandma Dixie, Grandpa Joe, Uncle Dale. I asked him, "What about them?" He answered, "I want Dixie. I want Joe." "What will you say when you see them?"

Nathan's answer was always the same: "I love you."

He soon learned that his endearing phrase could sometimes keep away punishment. When he heard a tone of voice that sounded displeased, he learned to quickly respond, "I love you."

No matter how many times Nathan tells me, I never get tired of hearing him say, "I love you." What a wonderful reminder. When was the last time you told the people who are dearest to you that you love them? When you don't have anything else to say, why don't you tell them you love them?

2. Live in the Now

Plans, clocks, calendars, schedules, checklists, shopping lists, remember everything, hurry, be on time, finish the project...

After I finish this project or chore, I can think about that. Just a minute, I'm busy. Later, later...

I have learned from Nathan, and I am constantly reminded by him, now, at the time we are together, to enjoy every moment. Look at the beautiful weather, the beautiful flowers, let us hug and talk to each other and look at each other while we are in the same room together.

He wants our whole family to be together, so when Daddy or his sister are not at home, he is constantly asking for them. (I am told that when I am not home, his conversation is often, "Mama. Mama. Mama."). When we are all together at home, he expands to Grandma, Grandpa and Uncle Dale. He knows how important it is for family to be together, and he wants us to be together now. What good is talking about being together in the past or future, if we are not together now? Are we so busy planning for the future that we forget to live right now? Are we so worried about what happened yesterday that we can't be happy today?

When we are watching a TV program or sporting event or a movie together, do we sit in silence, absorbed in our own worlds? Or do we interact with each other, letting each other know what scenes are touching us, what makes us mad or sad or happy? I have a tendency to get lost in a movie and then let my own thoughts take me somewhere else, to the point that I almost forget I am in a room with others. Yet, Nathan keeps reminding me, he is here with me, he loves me, he needs me. Perhaps he doesn't understand the story line of the movie we are watching, but he does understand that we are together right now – so please pass the popcorn.

Nathan has a limited concept of time. He reminds me to look at him now, to interact with him now, to enjoy what is happening right at this moment, that we can be happy with each other right now. His very favorite time is when we, as a family, plus Grandma Dixie, Grandpa Joe, and Uncle Dale, are all together around the dinner table. His abbreviation for the all-together family dinner is, "Turkey." Adapted from our traditional Thanksgiving and Christmas dinners, this one word represents his desire for us to all be together around the table. His family together and delicious food - what could be better?

A few years ago, we went to the beach for a vacation. I was so thrilled to be at one of my favorite places. My husband, Nathan and I were walking on the sand towards the beach when I asked Nathan, "Do you know were we are?" He nodded once as he answered enthusiastically, "Yeah. Right HERE!!"

Am I living RIGHT HERE? RIGHT NOW? Worrying about the future won't help, and living in the past can't change it.

Enjoy your day - now!

3. Make Known What You Want

How often do we hint or hedge around or just hope others will know what we want, without saying it? We perk up when we see a commercial on TV for something we want, we might leave a catalog or magazine open to a page showing an item we like, or we might assume others will read our minds and provide us with what we want. I have difficulty telling others what I want.

Nathan does not have this problem. Everyone he meets knows he wants ice cream. How do we know? Because he tells us. He often first tries the most abbreviated sentence: "I want ice cream," but that does not get results with us, his family, so then he makes his request a little more polite: "I want ice cream, please." My mother, his grandmother, does not accept this sentence, so the next phrase he learned after "I love you," was "May I have some ice cream, please?" He nods his head to each word, as if this request must be asked to the beat, so a word won't be left out. At Grandma's house, this is the polite phrase that often gets results.

Nathan doesn't always get ice cream, but people do understand his request. Some responses to his statement, "I want ice cream" have been: "So do I;" "That sounds good;" "You just had some;" or, "We all do." However, he never stops informing others of what he wants. Everybody knows Nathan wants ice cream.

Usually, he tells me what he wants using just one word: hamburger, pop, cake, movie. I remind him, "How do you ask for that at Grandma's house?" He responds while nodding his head for each word, "May I have some (***place item he wants here***), please?"

4. Praise God with Abandon

Nathan has always loved church. We have been taking him to church since he was a baby. We attend a Baptist church where the congregation makes no secret of loving God. Nathan gets excited and he is not afraid to show it. During the praise music and during the preaching, Nathan praises God with all of his body, his mind, and his soul. He reacts to the preaching and the music with all of himself, not holding anything back.

Before he was a year old, while sitting in his stroller at church, he began to watch my husband, the pastor, with fascination. He never misbehaved in church because he has always been involved with the service, paying attention to what is happening and imitating Daddy's hand movements. He began to hold his flashlight to his mouth like a microphone, with a handkerchief wrapped around it, just like Daddy.

When it is time to praise God, Nathan doesn't hold back. He claps, shouts, jumps up and down, unrestrained, happy, excited, joyful. He doesn't care who knows how much he loves Jesus. He praises God with all he has, with all he is.

Isn't this what God asks of us?

Many of us are too ashamed, embarrassed or too rigid to praise God with all that we are. We think, "God knows how I feel," or "God knows my heart." Yes, He does. He also knows that when we are holding in our praises, we care more about what other people think of us than what God thinks of us. He knows we are holding in our praises that rightly belong to Him, in order that we might not look foolish among people.

Do I praise God with all I have? Or am I more concerned with what others see me doing, what they might think? What is more important, how I give my praise to God, and what God thinks about me, or what other people see me do? I need to assume, like Nathan, that everyone in the sanctuary is as focused on praising God as I am, and they are not even paying attention to how I praise Him.

5. Be Happy

Nathan is the happiest person I know! He is always smiling, always excited about what we are doing, always spreading joy among everyone he meets. He is excited to see people and he shows his enthusiasm.

It's true, he doesn't have the worries that many of us have, about money, the future, and what people think of us. But, to put it simply, why are wasting our joy and happiness worrying about those things? Does worrying solve any problem or situation?

Whenever I have a concerned look on my face, Nathan notices and simply tells me, "Happy," reminding me to be happy right now.

This follows up to living in the Now. Be happy you are here now, doing what you are doing now, because now is the only time you can be happy. If you are waiting for things to be perfect before you can be happy, you will never be happy.

Look at Nathan! He is happy now and he is always happy.

6. Celebrate Small Victories

When a little boy completes a task for the first time, his parents are quick to clap and cheer for him, to encourage his behavior. "Good job!" "Good boy!" "That's right!" It is rewarding to us when Nathan finally accomplishes something, so we are very vocal and active in our approval, to let him know he is doing the right thing.

When Nathan was small, we lived in a house with steps to downstairs. We normally kept a gate across the top so he wouldn't fall down the steps. When he got a little bigger, we taught him how to go down the steps, first by crawling backwards, then by holding the rail and stepping down, one step at a time. One of us would always watch him as he carefully made his way to the bottom – and every time, he would give himself applause at the end.

When he learned and accomplished a new task, we continued to encourage him the second, third, fourth and fifth times, but after that, the task became routine. However, Nathan became accustomed to the cheering and applause, so he continued to cheer for himself. He put on his own hat. He clapped. He crawled down the steps and when he got to the bottom, he clapped. He went to the bathroom by himself. He clapped. He finished his food. He clapped.

After he got a little older, he didn't always applaud himself anymore, but he continued his self-encouragement by saying, "Good job," or, the abbreviated version, "Job." We still hear him in the other room saying, "Job," and we know as well as he does, he has done something right.

He makes me smile, reminding me to celebrate small victories, no matter how many times I have previously accomplished those tasks. I emptied the dishwasher! Finished paying the bills! Went shopping! Made dinner! Made the bed! Washed the car! When I stop to consider, many of those small tasks that I do almost automatically, some people are not able to do. I can do it and I did do it! Every victory, no matter how small, deserves to be celebrated.

How often do we celebrate our own small victories? When we complete a task we didn't want to do, or a large project we have worked on for a long time, do we take the time to celebrate our victories? I have learned from Nathan, it is important to acknowledge all victories in our lives, large and small, so the general attitude of our living does not become mundane, dreary, or ignored – by us. If we don't celebrate our own successes, milestones, and accomplishments, who will?

7. Ask for Help When You Need It

"Help, please." Nathan learned early to ask for help, shortly after he began saying words. He couldn't do much on his own, so he learned to ask us for help at home, and later ask for help at school. It came out more like "hep-pease," but we could tell what he meant. Sometimes at school his teacher said he asked for too much help, but at least he did ask; especially if he felt like he couldn't do something or needed to be shown how to do it.

I have difficulty asking people for help. Either I think I can do everything myself, no one is available, or I just don't know who to ask. Or perhaps I don't want people to know I can't do everything. In this area, I need to take a cue from Nathan. People are usually willing and even happy to help. Do you try to do everything on your own? Just ask for help.

8. Keep Trying Until You Succeed

When Nathan was six years old and in the first grade, every morning I helped him put on his socks. I showed him how to put both thumbs into one sock and pull it onto his foot, then I repeated showing him with the other sock. I told him what I was doing and showed him, every day for six months. I had been helping him get dressed all his life, and at this time, I was showing him and hoping and praying that he was paying attention. Each morning when he was getting dressed, he held up his socks to me and said, "Help, please." The next step, I put his thumbs into the sock and guided it onto his foot, but he still couldn't do it himself. I showed him and I told him what I was doing, every day.

One evening we were getting ready to go out to dinner. Nathan brought his socks to me while I was talking to my husband in the kitchen. Nathan held up his socks to me and said, "Help, please."

I told him, "Nathan, I have been showing you how to put on your socks for six months! You need to do it yourself! You need to put on your own socks!"

I turned back to the conversation with my husband while Nathan went into the dining room, carrying his socks. We were having a deep discussion (so important at the time, yet now I can't recall the subject) and had been talking for at least ten minutes when Nathan emerged from the dining room, applauding. He had put on his own socks! He had struggled for all that time, while we were not paying any attention to him, and he finally pulled on his socks by himself! He did not give up, even though it was difficult for him, and I was not helping him.

Do we feel like giving up when something is difficult? Do we expect someone else to do it for us? Keep trying! Nathan can do it and so can we.

9. Imitate Those You Love

Nathan loves to imitate his daddy preaching. He watches videos at home during the week of our church services, and he gets the live dose every Sunday. He has this down to a science. He knows exactly when to stomp his foot, when to wipe his mouth with a hanky, when to reach out with his hand. His learning process is that he watches the video once or twice, then he plays the video, listening to it while watching himself in the mirror. When I watch him, I can see that he is going right along with each movement Daddy is making, without even looking again at the video. Nathan loves to imitate those he loves.

When we sit, Nathan sits. When we stand, he stands. When I am working a puzzle, he goes and gets one of his puzzles to work on. When I tap my chin in thought, he taps his chin. When Grandpa Joe makes hand movements to emphasize a point, Nathan imitates those hand movements, smiling and laughing all the time. (He thinks his grandpa is such an entertaining and funny person.)

He also likes to imitate his sister. When she is drawing, he wants to draw. She is an accomplished artist, and he draws circles and loops and stick figures, but he wants to do what she is doing. When she sings, he screeches along with her on the high notes, growls through the low notes.

One time, Nathan and I were in the bathroom, getting ready to brush our teeth. Nathan was just tall as the counter. I saw a fruit fly on the mirror, so I slapped it with the palm of my hand. Nathan imitated me by slapping the counter, and I laughed, since he didn't know why I slapped the mirror. He was merely imitating me.

Nathan decided that was part of our teeth-brushing routine, and every night for the next few months he slapped the counter at that same spot when I handed his toothbrush to him.

Nathan can dress himself, but he still needs help with adjustments: getting his shoes on the right feet, pulling up the backs of his shoes, buttoning, putting on his tie and belt. One Sunday morning, I was helping with his shoes, and my finger got stuck in the back of the shoe when he stepped down on it. I loudly whispered, "Ouch." For the next few weeks, every time he put on a shoe, he whispered, "Ouch," just as he stepped down into the shoe, regardless if my finger was in it or not. He continually imitates the ones he loves.

It's been said that imitation is the most sincere form of flattery. Are we imitating the positive aspects of those whom we love most?

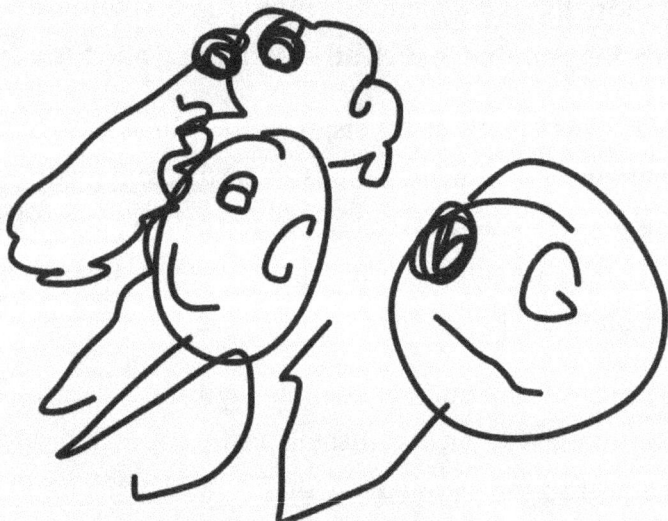

10. Forgive and Forget (Forgive means Forget)

When Nathan was four years old, we took a vacation in July to visit family members in California. We arrived at my cousin's house, which was enclosed with a tall fence. Behind the fence were ten wildly-barking dogs. Nathan was so excited, because he loves animals, and instead of being afraid of them, he was interacting with them through the fence. My cousin came to the gate and shouted to us over the barking that these were dogs he had rescued, and he would put them in the house, in the bedroom, before he opened the gate. The sound of barking became muffled and we entered the house, greeting and hugging my cousin and his wife.

Suddenly the barking grew frantic. Somehow, the dogs escaped! All ten charged over to where we were standing, barking in a frenzy. Nathan was at my side and the dogs seemed to focus on him as the smallest human, so I scooped him up just as he screamed. Two of the dogs were biting his leg! I tapped their noses and they backed off. My cousin and his wife again corralled all ten dogs and herded them back into the bedroom. Nathan's calf was torn open, so we wrapped it with a towel and prepared to take him to a doctor to get it checked. My cousin assured us that all the dogs had their rabies shots.

Since it was the afternoon of July 3ʳᵈ, the only doctor in the small town had already closed his office for the 4ᵗʰ of July holiday, so the only thing to do was to take Nathan to the emergency room at the nearest hospital. My cousin's wife accompanied us, and she brought the paperwork verifying the dates of the rabies vaccines. We arrived at the tiny emergency room, and probably because of the amount of blood soaking through the towel, he was checked in quickly and seen immediately after a stabbing victim, who was brought in by ambulance just after we arrived.

The doctor cleaned the wounds – Nathan had been bitten three times – and he used some kind of surgical tape to hold the skin together on the largest gash, then wrapped the entire calf with gauze. During this whole time, from the time we left the house until we left the hospital, Nathan did not cry. He was happy, smiling, and not complaining nor indicating he was in any pain. He was mildly interested in the wrap on his leg, but he was thrilled to be with us.

We returned to my cousin's house, where two of the dogs (friendly and non-barkers, non-biters) were out of the bedroom, the others still locked inside the bedroom. Nathan reached out to the two dogs and hugged them! If I had been bitten by dogs just a couple of hours earlier, I would not be able to embrace them, or even to welcome them. I would be terrified! But Nathan wasn't. He was so happy to see these dogs! He not only forgave dogs for biting him, he seemed to forget that dogs had been responsible for this great sore and bandage on his leg.

The next day, we drove to another cousin's house. She had three dogs, and Nathan was so loving to them. Here we were again with unfamiliar dogs, and Nathan was not holding anything against them. He still was a boy of very few words at this age. While we were sitting at the table eating dinner, Nathan removed himself from his chair. The rest of us watched him curiously. He walked to the front door and opened it, to let in one of the dogs that had inadvertently been locked outside. The dog scooted over to hide behind my cousin's legs, while Nathan simply climbed back into his chair, now ready to eat. Nathan and the dog had communicated. The rest of us had no idea that the dog was not in the house.

To this day, Nathan loves dogs. Whenever we approach any dog, I remind Nathan to stay back, don't touch, don't hug or kiss the dog. Are you able to forgive those who have hurt you? And then, can you forget, and move on, with love?

11. Don't Eat When You Are Full

Nathan is good at limiting how much he eats. Although he is a good eater, this is only when he is hungry. When he is not hungry, he doesn't eat. He won't eat just to be polite. He doesn't usually eat breakfast because he isn't hungry in the morning.

When he eats, he is hungry. When he is hungry, he can eat a lot. He has a good appetite and he eats just about any food served to him (including vegetables). However, when he is finished, he says, "All done," and he won't eat any more. He won't eat when he is bored, he won't eat when he is upset. He won't eat to please someone else. He only eats when he is hungry.

I think a lot of us in our society could do well to follow this example, myself included. I'm learning from you, Nathan!

12. Follow Directions Exactly

Nathan understands things literally, so he follows directions exactly. I have already mentioned that when I told him to just say hi and that's all to strangers, he would say hi, the stranger would say hi, and then Nathan would again say hi. Nathan was doing exactly as I had instructed him.

One time when Nathan was three, he was very excited to go somewhere with his sister and me. She and I weren't quite ready to go, so she told him, "Hold your horses." He went into his room for a minute and then he brought out two of his toy horses. He stood in the hall holding them until we were ready to go.

When I was teaching Nathan to brush his teeth, I finally got him to stop just chewing on his toothbrush, but he would only brush his lower teeth, brushing back and forth. I showed him how I was brushing my teeth, and I told him, "Go up and down." He stood there with his toothbrush in his mouth and bent his knees, straightened up, bent his knees and straightened. He was going up and down, just like I told him.

When Nathan was 18, I took him to get his ID card at the Department of Licensing. When we arrived, about 10 people were in line ahead of us. I had to use the restroom, so I asked Nathan to wait in line and to save my place and I would be right back. When I came out of the restroom, the line had moved ahead but Nathan was still standing in the same place. He pointed with both hands, palms up, to the floor where I had been standing, and shouted, with a huge smile on his face, "Here!" He had literally saved my place on the floor.

Last year, we were about to eat dinner and Nathan came to the table with just a white t-shirt on. My husband prefers for men at the table to wear a shirt over a white t-shirt, so he told Nathan to go put on another shirt. Nathan went to his room and came back in his white t-shirt. My husband told him again, "Go put on another shirt." Nathan returned to his room and came back to the dining room in a white t-shirt. His dad was losing patience with him – he had told him twice already – and Nathan whined with frustration when Daddy told him, "I said to put on another shirt." So, I went with Nathan to his room this time, asking him, "Don't you know what it means to put on another shirt?" When we got to his room, two white t-shirts were on his bed, wadded up, just removed. Nathan had indeed put on another shirt – another white t-shirt. His dad hadn't explained to put on a different shirt over his white t-shirt. Nathan had done just what he had been told to do – he put on another shirt.

Do we follow directions exactly? Or do we disregard instructions and do things our own way?

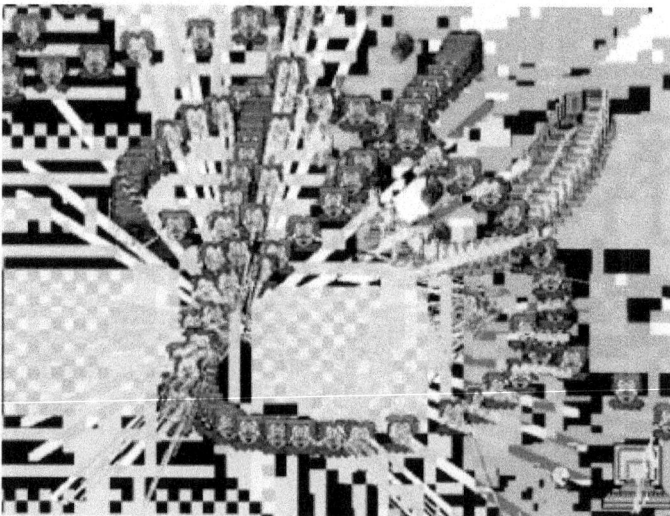

You should also know...

Nathan is now 22 years old as I am finishing this book.

What Nathan's grandfather did for him

Nathan is a very special member of our family. He is the happiest and most loving person I know. But if it had not been for my dad, Nathan's grandfather, Nathan would not have the life nor the freedom to do what he does today.

My dad, Joseph Fram, was the superintendent of a residential institution for severely disabled (known as 'retarded' back then) persons in the 1960s to the 1980s. He changed the way society looked at disabled persons by getting them out of their beds, letting them learn, integrate into society, and, if they were ready, move out of the institution.

My dad was the first to begin using an IEP, Individual Educational Program, for disabled students, with the theory that each person could learn and grow to his own potential. In the early 1960s, he worked with others and with Eunice Kennedy Shriver to create the Special Olympics. He came up with the concept of LRE, Least Restrictive Environment, for education and placement of special needs students. He worked with school districts to form classrooms to serve students who needed extra educational help but could live at home. He worked with others in the community to form the first group homes for disabled adults, and to create businesses that would hire adults with special needs. My dad lobbied to help get disabled persons the right to vote. Thousands of scientists, doctors and educators came from around the world to see the innovative work my dad was doing at this institution.

Nathan's grandfather made it possible for Nathan to live at home with us and go to public schools while he was growing up, instead of living in an institution. He made it possible for Nathan to compete in Special Olympics while attending a public school. He made it possible for Nathan to work at a job here in town, at a business established by my dad's good friend for this specific purpose: to employ people with special needs. Because of the things my dad did to help countless people around the globe with his new ideas, concepts and experimentations, my dad's grandson is able to live the life he has now.

My Appreciation

Thank you to everyone who has supported Nathan throughout his journey, especially Dr. Fuchs, Haley Farley (and your dad), Sam, Roderick, Crystal, Ms. Weigant, Linda Ayala, Randi Krieg, Randy Scott, Bethany, Brandy, and Preston. You have made all the difference in his life.

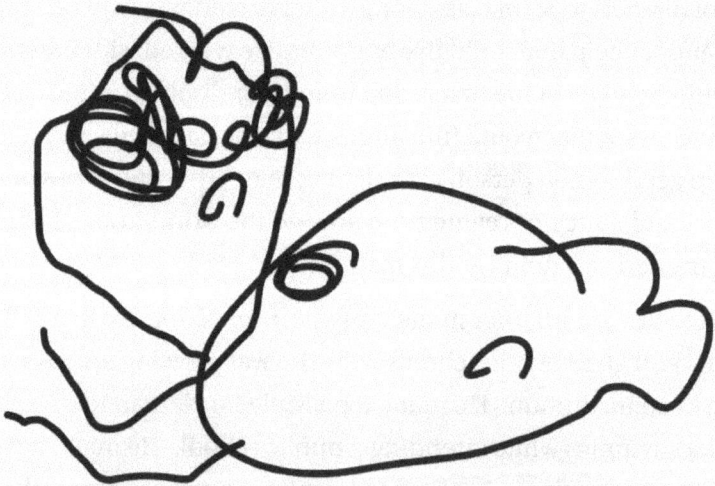

Also available from Everlasting Publishing

Nathan is Nathan
by Nathan's Sister

Nathan was born in 1998, and it wasn't too long before we noticed that Nathan cannot be compared to other kids. Nathan has Pervasive Developmental Disorder (PDD) in the autistic spectrum, and so he speaks, plays and learns differently than other kids. Nathan has trouble remembering how to say words, but he has a very good memory. He loves music and is a crazy dancer, he loves people and he does not ever stay mad. Even if he can't tell you, he understands when you talk to him.

With help, Nathan can become who he wants to be. Nathan thinks differently. Nathan learns differently. Nathan is simply Nathan.

Nathan Art: Autistic-Artistic
by Nathan

The art in this book was created by Nathan using the computer, while he was between the ages of 5 and 8. Nathan has ASD (Autistic Spectrum Disorder) - specifically, he has been diagnosed with PDD, Pervasive Developmental Disorder in the autistic spectrum. During the years when he was making these remarkable creations and the 120 other amazing pictures we have been able to retrieve from the computer, Nathan spoke very little. He struggles to say just a few words, often having a hard time remembering words. He uses sign language to help him communicate, both to prompt his speech and to convey his needs.

Although Nathan hasn't been able to tell us what is going on inside his mind, he has created many fantastic pictures using the computer. These are just a few.

Check out all our books at
everlastingpublishing.org

www.ingramcontent.com/pod-product-compliance
Lightning Source LLC
Chambersburg PA
CBHW071826020426
42331CB00007B/1619